Desmond's Birthday Surprise

Story and pictures

by Althea

Published by Dinosaur Publications

GW00338571

Desmond was on holiday with
the monsters at their big house in France.
It was summer and they could
play outside all day.

Mostly they played football but
they had lots of picnics too.

Soon it would be Desmond's birthday.
The monsters decided to give him
a special surprise party.

It needed a lot of planning and
they kept whispering about it together.
They said 'shush' to each other
whenever Desmond came along.

Poor Desmond was getting very worried.
Perhaps they don't like me any more,
tomorrow I will pack and go home,
he thought.

He was feeling rather sad
– so sad that he had forgotten
all about his birthday.

But the next morning he was woken up
by all the monsters singing
'Happy Birthday' to him.
Their voices were so loud that
probably everyone in the valley
was woken up too.

Desmond got lots of presents.
He kept saying 'Thank you.'
He had an extra long bath brush
so he could wash his back properly.
The brush was shaped like a goose.
Desmond rather hoped it would float
in his bath.

There was a big story book with lots
of stories and pictures, and
a drawing book and some paints
so Desmond could make his own pictures.

There were four roller skates.
Desmond was a bit worried about these
because he thought he would keep
falling over. He decided to wait and
try them later when no-one was looking.
He wondered what was in the other parcels.

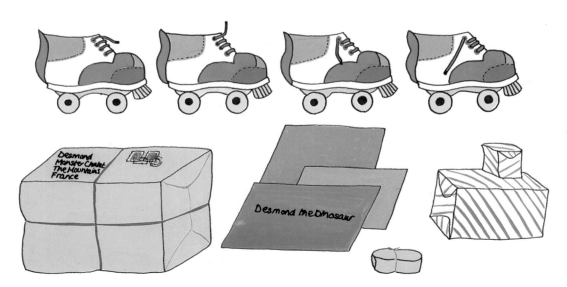

Then came the big party.
Everyone for miles around had
been invited.
Lots of people had brought food
and there was an enormous feast.

Soon the sky was bright with rockets and stars, flashing lights of red, blue, gold and silver.

I shall certainly remember that party for the next million years, thought Desmond, as he went to sleep that night.

They danced and played games
until evening. Desmond even had
a little go on his roller skates.
He only fell over twice.

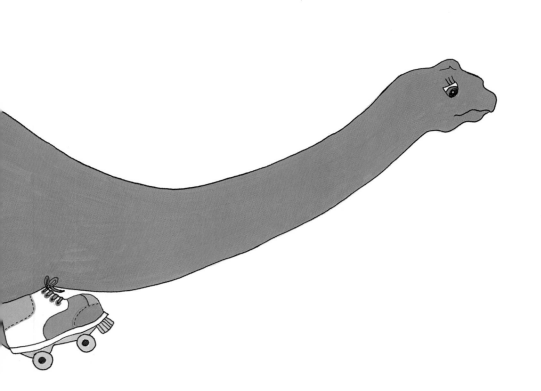

When it started to get dark
the monsters brought out the
enormous birthday cake they had made.

It had 75 candles on it, one for each million years of Desmond's life. It looked very bright.

day Desmond

Everyone cheered as Desmond
blew out all the candles
with one enormous puff.
He felt very proud and happy
as he made his secret wish.